An
Eight-Session
Anger
Management
Pull-Out
Program

TemperTamers

Kathryn Pearson

M.S., Licensed Psychologist

IEP
RESOURCES

Author Kathryn Pearson, M.S., Licensed Psychologist

Editor Tom Kinney
Graphic Design Sherry Pribbenow
Additional Art Tereza Snyder

ISBN 1-57861-148-2

AN IEP RESOURCES PUBLICATION

RESOURCES

P.O. BOX 930160   VERONA, WI 53593-0160
PHONE: 800-651-0954   FAX: 800-942-3865

Acknowledgements

I would like to acknowledge and thank the following people for their help and support.

Jonelle Klemz, B.S., LSW, Facility Facilitator with the Rum River Special Education cooperative for her good natured support and help in managing the groups.

Kathy Baker, Ed.S., Principal, Braham Elementary School for her dedication in providing creative ways to resolve children's problems.

Loretta Saylor, LICSW, Children's Mental Health Supervisor at Isanti County Family Services for her vision regarding early intervention and prevention.

The staff at **Braham Elementary School** for their enthusiasm.

Teresa Casey-Wolf, M.S.E., NCSP, Special Education Coordinator in the North Branch school district for her competent advice regarding IEP criteria.

Herman Jackson of Attainment Company, Inc. for his boundless energy and his ability to conceptualize.

My husband **Bill**, for encouraging me, and our sons, **Jesse**, **Sam** and **Micah** for their technical support.

About the Author

Kathryn Pearson

received her B.A. degree from Augsburg College, Minneapolis, and her M.S. degree in Counseling and Guidance from the University of Wisconsin-Madison.

Her career in psychology began by teaching assertiveness skills to student teachers for her Master's thesis. Over the years she has worked with a wide variety of populations, including: At a college campus, an adult residential treatment facility, community and county mental health centers and in private practice. Currently she provides therapy and consults in schools and works in a hospital-based clinic providing mental health services to children and adults.

Pearson was raised in Japan by her missionary parents. She credits this bicultural background for her ability to understand the perspectives of others and to translate that into stories which are meaningful to them.

She lives with her husband Bill, a Lutheran minister and their three sons.

Pearson can be contacted for training/workshops at: tempertamers@qwest.net, or call 763-689-3750.

photo by V.S. Arrowsmith

Table of Contents

Acknowledgements   3

About the Author   4

Introduction   6

Session One   17

Session Two   31

Session Three   39

Session Four   49

Session Five   59

Session Six   67

Session Seven   75

Session Eight   81

Appendix   93

Introduction

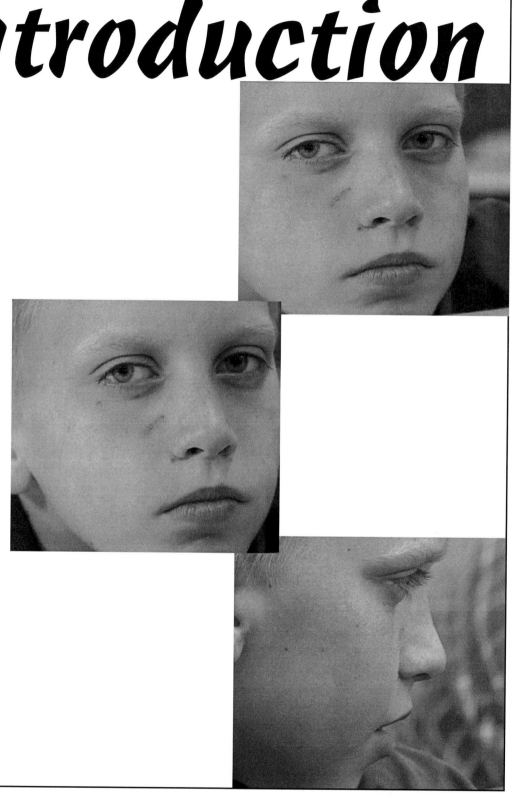

In my work as a psychologist in private practice,

I've seen a steady increase in referrals of children who struggle with managing their anger, and over the years I've come up with three basic strategies to help them help themselves:

1. by helping them sort out their feelings;

2. by helping them express feelings once recognized; and

3. by helping them chart a course of action to avoid getting into trouble.

Then, several years ago I began working in an elementary school where a similar phenomenon was occurring: i.e., increasing numbers of students being referred because of anger management problems. In the school setting, I've found that small group work is the most efficient and is very effective.

This book is the result of both areas of experience — therapy in the private and public sectors — and takes a step-by-step behavioral approach to teaching anger management strategies to small groups of young children in school settings. I have found that I can also adapt the material for use in private practice with one child and I've been able to adapt it for use in a grade-wide curriculum with entire classrooms as well.

The first step and most important building block is to teach children to identify their emotions so that when they become angry they are aware of it and can self-implement coping strategies. Many children are not aware of their emotions beyond the ones most easily identified — happy, sad, mad. Initially, this curriculum teaches children to name the feelings they have in response to certain situations (i.e., lonely, frustrated, jealous). When they have become proficient at this, they explore their anger, which is explained to them as a legitimate and natural emotion that occurs as a response to a variety of often unpredictable and unavoidable circumstances. Everyday situations, in other words, that are bound to occur in every child's life and for which he or she should have some preparation.

Children who have been referred for anger management problems instantly react in destructive and socially inappropriate ways when angered. Unfortunately, our culture too often promotes aggressive behaviors as the only legitimate response to anger. You need look no further than the runaway popularity of professional wrestling in which violence, acted out in a stagy and larger-than-life fashion, is always the only answer to insults, to perceived slights or to the smallest of disagreements.

This behavioral program teaches children how to respond when they are angry so they do not have to get into trouble by hurting people or by destroying things. Children who can successfully harness their emotions — especially their angry ones — are more likely to have a positive self image and increased self-esteem.

Having said this, realize that there will be some kids — who are just too angry, who have too many other pressing issues — for whom the small group approach (recommended here) will not work and is not appropriate. This program does not pretend to be a panacea for all kids, including those who are extremely involved, and should not be seen as such.

It's a monumental challenge to teach alternative ways to respond to anger which involve cognitive and behavioral change. It's also imperative that we do so and quickly, because children are being injured and worse as a result of inappropriate expressions of anger.

The referral process comes from school personnel: Classroom teachers, building principals, title staff, paraprofessionals. Some will also come from parents. However the referrals arrive, you will have to secure the consent of parents, in writing, to have their children involved in the group. It's helpful for the group leader to explain a little about **TemperTamers** to the parents. This is followed up with a permission slip for their child to participate. A reproducible Parent Permission Form is included on page 15.

Because elementary school children have a fairly short attention span, and these groups are conducted as pull-outs during the school day, they are designed to take from 30 to 45 minutes per session.

Group size and other considerations

- keep group numbers at no higher than six to eight children.

- keep a balance in each group, making sure you don't get too many tough kids in one group . . . if necessary, divide the most challenging students and make a second group.

- although TemperTamers is appropriate for students grades 1-6, form your groups roughly by age, (e.g., grades 2–3).

- have one group leader and one adult helper. (This is important because the content of the group will arouse the children's emotional responses, and having an extra adult to help with discipline will save your group from chaos.)

- make sure you have a table, preferably a round one that all of the children can sit around, to accommodate all the hands-on activities, many of which require a writing space.

How TemperTamers Works

The program includes eight group sessions, each of which follows a sequenced format: Homework review, a mini-lecture, TemperTamer stories, learning activities, and a presentation of next week's homework.

Homework

The homework component consists of keeping a very brief log of instances when students became angry and how they've dealt with it. It's somewhat challenging, but necessary, because it insures carryover from our discussions to their daily lives. A small reward for completion is incentive enough to gain their compliance. At the beginning of each session, each child has the opportunity to recount a story taken from their homework sheet, which is a key component in allowing for a generalization of skills learned during group. (As is the case with all mandated reporters working in a school setting, there may be occasions when children describe incidents which require reporting.)

Mini-lecture

Each session includes at least a few mini-lectures. These are instructor prompts that provide you with instructions for the students in your pull-out group. Talented group leaders will soon come up with their own versions once they become familiar with the steps of the program, but these will give you a helpful starting place.

Stories and Activities

There are three key concepts operating in TemperTamers:

1. the use of the stories;

2. the StopLight Solution; and

3. an Assertiveness MiniCourse.

Below I will briefly explain the rationale for each one:

1. The Story Approach

In my experience, the best way for maintaining the interest of children this age — and the linchpin of this program — is the use of stories offering a "point of view" perspective. Each session includes several TemperTamers stories that allow students to see the lesson in the context of a real life situation. As the program progresses, students are taught specific anger management strategies they can use when needed. Each strategy is imbedded in a story which makes its use clear. It follows the theory of ancient tribal instruction: "attach information to emotion for memory's sake." In other words, by animating the emotional content of each story with point of view characters, students remember the point of the lesson. This lesson is reinforced in the activity for each session.

Stories featured in the last several sessions illustrate how anger management strategies (taught in the activities) provide rewarding results for the child who uses it. For example, story characters use "breathing" techniques to relax when they're about to explode, or practice "stop and think" tactics.

Research has proven the use of point of view stories — sometimes called "bibliotherapy" — to be an effective approach for reaching young students about sensitive and hard to discuss issues, according to author and professor Dr. Sheldon Braaten: "Bibliotherapy is a very good strategy for making points with younger children, because it allows them to depersonalize the critical information being presented. Otherwise, kids are often uncomfortable talking about their own behaviors. By talking about other people, or relating to characters in stories kids can get enough distance from their own feelings to give them a comfort zone."

A more recent term for a very similar approach to bibliotherapy is "emotional literacy," an introduction to primary emotions for young children that also uses a storytelling approach. For example, a story character will display an envious response to a situation to illustrate the emotion "jealousy."

Each group meeting centers around several stories that directly relate to the behavioral goal of that session. Every teacher knows that children become more attentive when they are read engrossing stories. One only needs to recall images of a masterful storyteller who can keep large numbers of elementary school children enraptured in their school media center to recognize the power of the spoken word. I have found that children seem to settle down, tune in and process the information in a productive fashion when the TemperTamers stories are read to them. (All TemperTamer stories are fictional.)

2. The StopLight Solution

Sessions 4, 5 and 6 introduce a technique to help students deal with anger outbursts that is designed to be simple, and once mastered can be used in any situation. It's called The StopLight Solution. Once taught, students are able to mediate their initial response to the anger emotion by visualizing a stoplight and following three steps, each corresponding to the changing colors of a traffic light:

a. **Stop** = red — students learn to recognize (to stop) when they are angry and take a deep breath;

b. **Think** = yellow — students learn to plan (to think out) a solution for dealing with their anger; (Note: This part of the program helps children with cognitive restructuring, and in Session 4 they begin to learn how to process alternative ways to handle situations like, "I don't always get to do what I want," or, "Sometimes things aren't fair, I don't want to get into trouble.")

c. **Go** = green — students learn to implement (to go) their solution. (Note: Some children may never get past the red stop and breathe concept. And they won't be "cured" in eight weeks (see Reality Check section on next page) but through exposure to this information some advanced learning will take place. Consider this: How many adults can always stop their anger reactions, form a plan of action and implement it successfully?)

The third step, "Green = go," leads into the third key component of TemperTamers, the Assertiveness MiniCourse.

3. Assertiveness MiniCourse

A significant early part of my background as a psychologist has been spent in the field of assertiveness training. However, when teaching young children assertiveness skills in a small group setting, it is necessary to translate the traditional therapeutic language. For example, if working with adults, I would talk about aggressive, passive and assertive behaviors. But these words don't register with kids grades 1–6. In Session 6, we introduce as alternate terms "shouting" (= aggressive), "pouting" (= whiny, passive) and "no doubting" (=indecisiveness vs. being assertive). These alternative terms allow them to identify these behaviors in themselves. It has been my experience that most of the students in this pull-out group relate to these terms and that they already have been exhibiting all three of these behaviors.

The "green" segment of the Stoplight Solution involves teaching these assertiveness skills to students in your group.

Assertive behaviors are taught in Session 7 by showing students how to STAND STRONG and how to SPEAK STRONG. This includes body language, tone of voice and the student's ability to discriminate when he is using, or not using these techniques.

It's also important that throughout the program, teachers frequently remind the students that just because we act appropriately doesn't mean that others will change their behaviors. Sometimes they will, sometimes not, but it's still important for us to do the right thing.

Reality Check

Since each person's response to the feeling of anger is a learned reaction, you know already that you shouldn't expect highly aggressive children to be "cured" after attending an eight week group. However, it's a start. And with repetition, continued exposure, a climate and a culture conducive to mediating violent reactions, children can be taught to decrease aggressive outbursts. If the terminology, concepts and visual prompts used in this curriculum were adopted on a school wide basis, I believe there would be a far greater likelihood of significant and permanent behavior change. Included in the reproducible materials are pre-and post-group questionnaires to be filled out by a classroom teacher or parent to determine if change has actually occurred.

TemperTamers is appropriate for any student who needs extra work on anger management skills. It's likely that some, if not most, of the students will already be identified as having special needs and may already by experiencing pull-outs for other reasons. However, many students who need this class will not come from special education. For those who are identified kids, each session has a primary goal that allows you to attach results to student IEPs. Easy-to-use IEP attachment reproducibles are on pages 12-14.

Turn for IEPs

Three reproducible IEP pages provide ready-to-go attachments that can be added to any behavioral program for students with special needs. They include annual goals and the necessary benchmarks with which they can be attained. IEP materials are found on the following three pages.

IEP

Student Name _____

Date _____

Annual Goal

1 of 3

_____ will learn to identify emotions leading to his/her anger as measured by data on a pre- and post-group test, following participation in an 8 week emotions-anger group.

Short Term Objectives or Benchmarks

_____ will learn to identify a variety of emotions including negative and uncomfortable ones as evidenced by completion of activities and homework sheets in sessions 1 and 2.

_____ will learn to identify what makes him/her angry as evidenced by completion of activities and homework sheets in session 3.

_____ will learn to identify cues to how his/her body feels when angered as evidenced by completion of activities in session 3.

IEP

Student Name _____

Date _____

Annual Goal

2 of 3

_____ will learn to moderate his/her anger and will learn management techniques to control it as measured by data on a pre- and post- group test following participation in an 8 week emotions-anger group.

Short Term Objective or Benchmarks

_____ will learn to stop escalating when he/she is angry as evidenced by completion of activities and homework sheet in session 4.

_____ will learn an appropriate course of action to use when angry as evidenced by completion of activities and homework in session 5.

_____ will learn to dispel aggressive energy as evidenced by completion of activities in session 8.

IEP

Student Name _____

Date _____

Annual Goal

3 of 3

_____ will learn to replace passive or aggressive behaviors with assertive behaviors as measured by data on a pre- and post-group test following participation in an 8 week emotions-anger group.

Short Term Objectives or Benchmarks

_____ will identify the difference between passive, aggressive and assertive behaviors as evidenced by completion of activities and homework sheets in sessions 5, 6, 7 and 8.

_____ will be able to demonstrate the ability to behave in an assertive manner when angered as evidenced by completion of activities and homework sheets in sessions 6, 7 and 8.

Parent Permission Form

We would like to offer your child an opportunity to be part of a small group. The group will work on helping children identify their emotions and then helping them deal with certain ones, like anger, that sometimes get them in trouble. The group will meet once a week for 30-45 minutes for 8 weeks.

The group will be led by _____

_____.

If you would like your child to participate, please fill out and return the permission slip below.

- -

Please detach and return

_____

I give permission for my child _____

to participate in the emotions group offered at _____

Parent/Guardian _____

Date _____

Pre- and Post-Test

What it does

The Pre- and Post-Test indicates where there is an increase in target behaviors. It will measure the students' ability to verbalize emotions, mediate anger and implement assertive behaviors.

Pre- and Post-Test

Dear Teacher,

Would you please fill out a pre-test (a post-test will follow after the group is completed) to help us determine if the anger-emotions (TemperTamers) group was effective? (Circle the appropriate response.)

1. Is student able to identify emotions by verbalizing a variety of emotions including anger?

1	*2*	*3*
rarely	sometimes	often

2. Is student able to calm him/her self down when angry?

1	*2*	*3*
rarely	sometimes	often

3. Is student able to implement an appropriate course of action which is neither passive or aggressive when angered?

1	*2*	*3*
rarely	sometimes	often

Session *One*

Goal

To help children identify a variety of feelings.

Materials

1. Feelings handout. Make one copy for each student. *page 25*

2. Feelings flashcard game. Make these ahead of time by reproducing the feelings flashcard pages and cutting them to make cards. (These could be laminated for extra durability.) *page 26*

3. Blank faces page/something to draw with (crayons, pencils, etc.). *page 29*

4. Session 1 TemperTamer stories. *page 20*

5. Session 1 homework sheet. *page 30*

Procedure

Since this is the first session it's a good time to establish ground rules such as: Respecting each other by listening when someone is talking, not talking to other students about information from the group (and other rules, as necessary). A group name can be established during this session (the children in the groups I have led enjoy identifying with their membership in the "**cool club**," and other age appropriate names will also work. The homework also needs to be explained at this time. Introduce it, emphasizing that it's the "easiest" homework they will ever be assigned and everyone who turns it in will receive a reward.

1. Mini-Lecture

After the initial business has been taken care of, say, "We're going to be spending some time together each week learning about feelings." Ask, "What are some of the different feelings that people can have?" Accept their answers and give each child a copy of the "Feelings Handout." Say, "Here are some more feelings that people can have." Read the ones that haven't been covered out loud.

2. TemperTamer Stories

Explain that you are going to be reading some stories and need the students to help identify the feelings that the children in the stories have. Then read the Session 1 stories and end with the fill-in-the-blank pause for the children to identify the feeling at the end of each story.

3. Activity

You will need the "Feelings Flashcards" for this activity. Explain that next you will play a game and the object is to name the feeling on the card that is being held up. Cover up the feeling word with your thumb or finger and give that card to the person who named the feeling. Students may refer to their own "feelings" handout for help. Every child can have the opportunity to be successful at least once in the game because several feelings can be attributed to the same expression.

4. Activity

Hand out the "Blank Faces" sheet and ask the children to draw a face in each one and to write down the feeling next to it. After they are finished, have a discussion and ask them to explain what they have drawn and why the person might have been feeling the way they were.

5. Homework

Hand out the homework sheets and explain that "for the easiest homework in the world," all they need to do is draw in the 3 circles with a feeling they felt and bring it to group next time.

Story 1

Best Friend's Birthday

Jordan was invited to his best friend's birthday party. When he went home to ask his mom if he could go, she said, "Yes," he could go and he could spend the night! He feels _____.

TemperTamer Stories

Story 2

Tanika's Grandma

Tanika just heard that her grandma is very sick and might die. Tanika loves her grandma very much.

She feels _____.

TemperTamer Stories

Story 3

Home Alone

Gretchen is home alone. She is watching TV and an announcement comes on the TV saying that a tornado is coming and people should go down to their basements. She doesn't know when her mom or dad are coming home. She feels_____.

TemperTamer Stories

Story 4

Tony's Present

Tony's uncle is coming to visit. His uncle brings everyone in the family a present. He brings Tony's brother a very fast remote control car. He brings his sister a Barbie Doll set with five different outfits. He brings his other brother a play station with three games. He brings Tony a tiny little bouncy ball. Tony feels _____.

TemperTamer Stories

Story 5

Fishing Trip

Manuelito can't wait until school gets out. His dad told him that the first weekend after school got out he would take him camping. Manuelito is already thinking about fishing and wants to check his tackle box to see what kind of lures he needs to buy before they go. He feels _____.

Feelings Handout

Visuals are a vital component in helping children understand their emotions. Each face represented on pages 26-28 (examples below) are included in reproducible form in the appendix starting on page 93. Take note that the facial expression of some feelings are virtually interchangeable — e.g., frustrated vs. stressed, sad vs. disappointed. Point this out to your students when introducing this session. This is useful information that allows them to become more "emotionally intelligent" and to better control their tempers.

calm	loving	happy	proud	excited	hyper
surprised	shy	bored	worried	confused	lonely
disappointed	upset	embarrassed	sad	mad	annoyed
stressed	frustrated	scared	rejected	jealous	nervous
guilty	furious	relieved			

Feeling Flashcards 1

Photocopy Feelings Flashcards and cut out.
They can also be laminated.

calm

loving

happy

proud

excited

stressed **3**

surprised **1**

shy **2**

bored **2**

Feeling Flashcards 2

Photocopy Feelings Flashcards and cut out.
They can also be laminated.

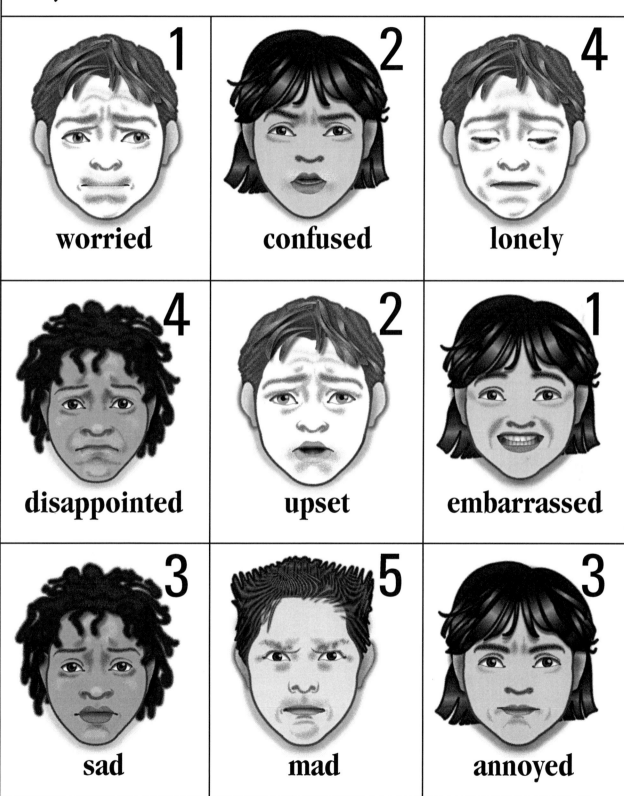

1 worried	2 confused	4 lonely
4 disappointed	2 upset	1 embarrassed
3 sad	5 mad	3 annoyed

Feeling Flashcards 3

Photocopy Feelings Flashcards and cut out.
They can also be laminated.

5 frustrated	3 scared	4 rejected
4 jealous	1 nervous	5 guilty
5 furious	hyper	relieved

Blank Faces Page

Homework Sheet

Draw 3 faces of 3 different feelings that you had.

Session
Two

Goal

To help children identify uncomfortable feelings.

Materials

1. Session 2 stories. *page 34*

2. Feelings Flashcard game from Session 1. Use only the numbered cards for this game. *pages 26-28*

3. Session 2 Homework sheet. *page 38*

Procedure

1. Review homework

Ask each group member to describe a feeling they had last week and reward the children who participate. You may want to promise the reward and then give it at the end of group time so the children won't be distracted by it.

2. TemperTamer Stories

Pause at the end to wait for the response with the feeling describing how the character feels.

3. Mini-Lecture

Say, "Last week we talked about all of the different feelings people can have which include: Proud, happy, sad, mad. Today we'll talk about uncomfortable feelings that people can have." Ask, "What are some of those uncomfortable feelings?" Wait for responses and then show the Session 2 Feelings Flashcards (the numbered ones), reading through them. Say, "Can you help it if you have an uncomfortable feeling – if something bad happens, for instance?" Then say, "No, we can't help having any of our feelings, they just happen."

4. Mini-Lecture/Activity

Say, "We're going to play a game using the Feelings Flashcards." Place the cards face down on the table and spread them all out. Say, "We will go around the circle and each person will pick up 2 cards to see if they have matching numbers. When you get a match, you get to keep the 2 cards and you have to tell a time when you had one of those feelings." (If children have difficulty telling a time when they had a feeling, they can be coached. It will not be hard to find a matching pair of numbers because the cards are numbered from one to five and there are four cards each with the same number.) If no match is found, the cards are placed back face down again and the next person gets to try. The game continues this way until all the cards are picked up. If you have additional time, students can describe when they felt the other emotion of their numbered pair. The purpose of the game is to provide a springboard for discussion about feelings and doing it in the context of the game is less threatening than to have an open discussion about feelings.

5. Homework

Hand out the Session 2 Homework sheets and ask the students to draw faces in the 3 circles that show an uncomfortable feeling each had during the week. Examples of the feelings could be: Sad, angry, scared, lonely, worried, disappointed, etc.

TemperTamer Stories

Story 1

What's the hurry?

TreShawn is hurrying because he doesn't have much time before the school bus comes. And he hasn't even had breakfast yet. His mom is rushing him saying, "Tre, hurry up and eat, the bus is coming!" So he is trying to gulp his cereal down as fast as he can. But when he reaches across the table for the cereal box his arm brushes against his juice cup, spilling it on his lap and getting his school pants all wet. TreShawn feels _____.

TemperTamer Stories

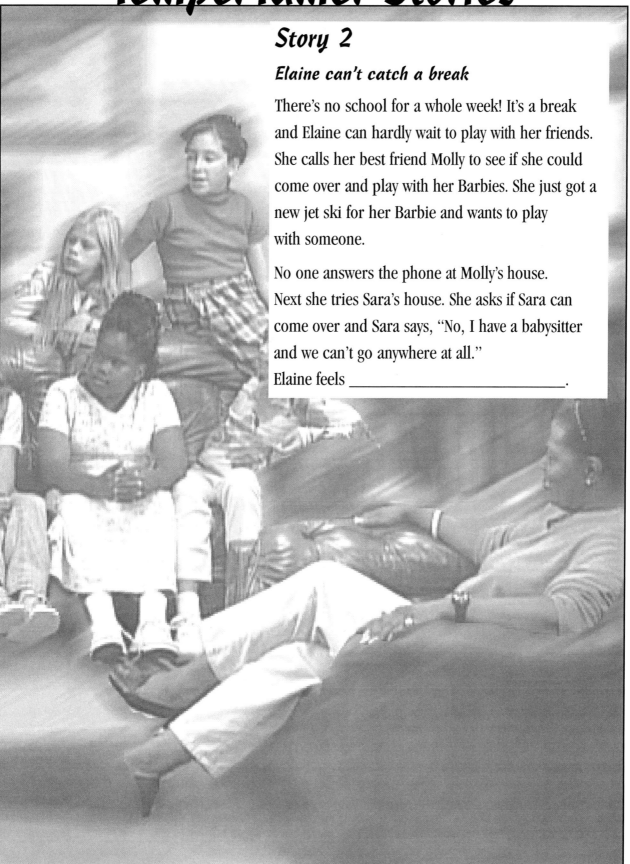

Story 2

Elaine can't catch a break

There's no school for a whole week! It's a break and Elaine can hardly wait to play with her friends. She calls her best friend Molly to see if she could come over and play with her Barbies. She just got a new jet ski for her Barbie and wants to play with someone.

No one answers the phone at Molly's house. Next she tries Sara's house. She asks if Sara can come over and Sara says, "No, I have a babysitter and we can't go anywhere at all."

Elaine feels _____.

Story 3

Michael's new puppy

Spike is nice, but he doesn't stay in the yard very well. So Spike has to be on a leash because the road in front of Michael's house is busy he could get run over. One day, Michael was just about to take Spike off the leash and put him back in the kennel when Spike broke free to chase a squirrel. Spike was chasing the squirrel and it was running right towards the road!

Michael felt _____.

TemperTamer Stories

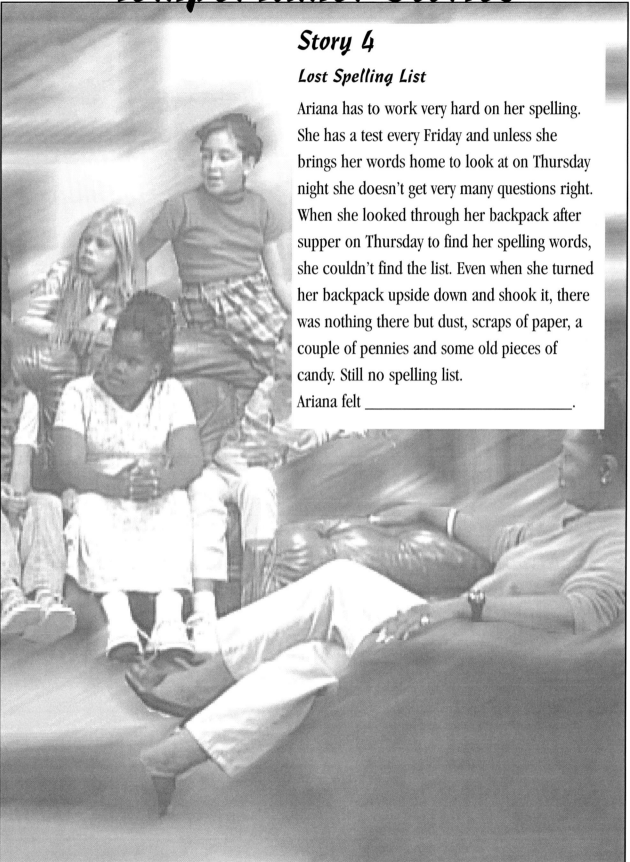

Story 4

Lost Spelling List

Ariana has to work very hard on her spelling. She has a test every Friday and unless she brings her words home to look at on Thursday night she doesn't get very many questions right. When she looked through her backpack after supper on Thursday to find her spelling words, she couldn't find the list. Even when she turned her backpack upside down and shook it, there was nothing there but dust, scraps of paper, a couple of pennies and some old pieces of candy. Still no spelling list.

Ariana felt _____.

Homework Sheet

Draw 3 faces of uncomfortable feelings that you had.

Session
Three

Goal

To help children identify what makes them angry and how anger makes their bodies feel.

Materials

1. Session 3 TemperTamer Stories. *page 42*

2. Session 3 Examples of What Makes us Mad Sheet. *page 45*

3. Boy and Girl Outlines, red crayons. *pages 46 & 47*

4. Session 1 Homework sheet. *page 48*

Procedure

1. Review homework

2. Mini-Lecture

Say, "What kinds of things make us angry?" and wait for a response. After some responses say, "Now we're going to read some stories about what made some kids angry."

3. TemperTamer Stories

Read the stories and wait for the response at the end.

4. Mini-Lecture

Say, "What other kinds of things could make us mad?" Wait for responses and then read Session 3 Examples of What Makes Us Mad Sheet. Ask after each example if that would make them mad.

5. Activity

Ask for volunteers to pantomime anger. Body language to include if they are having trouble: Angry facial expression; arms folded across chest; hands on hips; a rigid, seated posture with legs crossed; pointing fingers or other examples that come to mind.

6. Activity

Hand out outline of a boy or a girl (Session 3 Boy/Girl Outline). Say, "We can feel angry feelings in different parts of our bodies. When we feel angry feelings in our hands it might make us feel like hitting. If we feel them in our feet we might feel like kicking. If we feel them in our heads we might feel like we have a tight head or we might have a headache. Sometimes angry feelings make us not think clearly or feel confused. Angry feelings in our face might make us feel like shouting. Angry feelings in our stomach might give us a stomach ache." Hand out red crayons and ask students to color in on the outline where they feel it in their bodies when they get mad. Time permitting, ask children to explain their drawing after they have colored it.

7. Homework

Hand out the homework and ask the children to draw three faces of when something made them mad.

TemperTamer Stories

Story 1

Broken Horse

Bobby worked very hard during art, making a little horse out of clay. It needed to dry for one day before it could be painted. A mean kid in Bobby's class smashed his horse on purpose on the floor. Bobby felt

_____.

TemperTamer Stories

Story 2

Jasmine's Worksheet

Jasmine was paying attention to finishing the last answers on her worksheet and trying not to let Emily interrupt her. Emily was so annoying! She always thought she had the right answers. She sat in the desk behind her and was peeking at Jasmine's answers. Suddenly Emily stood up and grabbed Jasmine's worksheet and said, "Here, this is how to do it," and started to write on her paper. Jasmine felt _____.

TemperTamer Stories

Story 3

The Backpack

Juan got on the bus with a special treat in the back pocket of his backpack. He'd been shopping with his mom the day before and she didn't usually let him buy this snack. So he was excited and he could hardly wait to eat it during snack time. When he got to his seat, Juan put his backpack on the seat next to him, like he usually did. The next thing he knew, the kid who sat behind him grabbed his backpack and started throwing it around to tease him. Finally, the treats fell out and the mean kid grabbed them and wouldn't give them back. Juan felt _____.

Examples of What Makes us Mad

1. You hear a kid on the playground saying you're dumb.

2. You sneak a candy bar out of the cupboard and your brother tells on you.

3. You really want to watch your show on TV and your dad says you can't watch anymore.

4. You just got glasses and your friends are laughing at you, saying you look weird.

5. You don't understand your worksheet and the teacher says you have to stay after until you get it done.

6. Your friend got a prize on a coloring contest and you worked very hard to do a good job on your picture but you didn't get a prize.

7. Some kids are getting together after school but they didn't ask you to.

8. Your dad is moving out of the house because he doesn't get along with your mom anymore.

Girl Outline

Boy Outline

Homework Sheet

Draw 3 faces of when something made you mad.

Session *Four*

Goal

To help children to stop escalating when they are angry.

Materials

1. Session 4 Stories. *page 52*

2. Session 4 Handout: What to Do During the Think Step. *page 54*

3. Session 4 Activity Sheet. *page 55*

4. Session 4 Stoplight Handout; red, yellow and green crayons. *page 56*

5. Session 4 Homework. *page 57*

Leader Note

This session will introduce the concept of the stoplight, which has three basic components: red, stop and breathe; yellow, think, and green, go. This session will focus on red and yellow. Students will learn to mediate their initial rush of anger emotion by visualizing a stoplight and taking a deep breath. Then, they will be able to think of a plan under the yellow light. Sessions 5, 6, and 7 will show us how to carry out an appropriate plan of action and implement it, following the green light.

Procedure

1. Review homework

2. Mini-Lecture

Say, "It's not wrong to become angry because lots of things make us angry." Ask, "Would it be wrong to feel angry if someone did something bad to you?" Answer, "No, it's not wrong to feel angry but it is wrong to hurt someone or destroy something when you feel angry." Say, "We're going to learn a trick to use when we feel ourselves and our bodies getting angry." Say, "We're going to think of a stoplight, and what do all cars have to do when they see a red light? They have to stop. That's the same as what we need to tell our minds when something makes us angry. We're going to think of the red stoplight and "STOP."

After we think of "STOP" then we're going to take a deep breath through our nose and out our mouth. That breath will pull oxygen into our brain and help us control our temper so we don't do something that will get us into trouble." Say, "Let's practice taking a breath — in through the nose, and out through the mouth." Have each child practice breathing in through the nose and out the mouth.

3. TemperTamer Stories

Read Session 4 stories and go through the discussion questions.

4. Activity

Hand out the Session 4 Stoplight and the red, yellow and green crayons. Say, "Color the first light red and the next light yellow green." Say, "The red means to stop and the yellow means to think. We're going to think of some plans so we don't get in trouble when something makes us mad." Say, "You may color in the green when you're done." Say, "These are some things we can tell ourselves when we get mad." Distribute the session 4 Handout and read the suggestions out loud.

5. Activity

Next have the children pick 1 strip of paper (out of a hat or envelope), which has a scenario printed on it from Session 4 Activity Sheet. Have them read it or help them read the scenario and think of what they can tell themselves. Refer back to the Session 4 Handout for possible suggestions – Hint: Each number on the Handout corresponds with the number on the Activity Strip.

6. Homework

Hand out Session 4 homework saying, "Put down 3 different times that you got mad and stopped and breathed."

Story 1

Allen and the Grilled Cheese Sandwich

Allen just got home when his mom asked him if he had any homework to do. He had two worksheets to do, so he said he had a little. His mom said, "Good, because if you get it done, we can go roller skating with our friends, the Pattersons. They invited us and will come by to pick us up at 6:30." Allen was really looking forward to going roller skating. He had a snack and then turned on the TV to watch Pokemon. After Pokemon was over he looked outside and saw his friends playing football. They saw Allen watching them and called him to come out and join them. He asked his mom if he could and she said, "Sure, but only if you've finished your homework." He said, "Yea, mom, I'm done, can I go out?" She said, "Yes," and he went running out to play. It was great, he had so much fun. His team got the first touchdown. Then the other team scored, then his team scored again. Pretty soon the sun started to go down and the other boys had to go in to eat. He could hear his mom calling for him, too. She said, "Hurry up and eat this tomato soup, I forgot about the time — we have to hurry because they will be here any minute to pick us up to go roller skating! Here, show me your homework quick so I can check it." Allen looked at his mom and looked at the floor. "Uh, mom, I didn't have time to do it." She just looked at him and said, "Oh no, I guess you won't be able to go, will you?" Allen said, "Please mom, please I'll get it done when we get home, I promise!" His mom said, "No, you didn't do it — oh, here they are now. I'll have to tell them to go without you." Allen felt so mad he felt like exploding. He started to yell and threw his grilled cheese sandwich across the room where it smacked into the wall leaving a greasy stain.

Discussion

1. Is Allen going to get into trouble?

2. What made him mad?

3. How was he feeling?

4. What could he have done instead?

Story 2

Super Hungry Pabitra

Pabitra could hardly wait for lunch. Finally it was time to eat and her whole class got in line. They were having cheeseburgers, her favorite! When it was her turn, she got her burger, fries, carrot sticks and chocolate pudding. But she still needed her milk and because it was in the bottom of the bin she held her tray carefully in one hand and reached down. While she did that, her friend Toya, who was right behind her, bumped her hard and Pabitra's tray went flying, sending her lunch all over the place! The burger went one way and the fries went the other, while the carrots landed on the lunchroom lady's computer. Pabitra was embarrassed and she was mad, too, because she saw Toya laughing at her. And she didn't even apologize for bumping into her. Pabitra started to feel really angry. She could feel it in her legs and she just wanted to kick so she kicked her tray that had fallen on the floor and sent it crashing across the lunchroom.

Discussion

1. Will Pabitra get into trouble?

2. What was she feeling?

3. What could she have done instead of kicking her tray?

Handout

What to do during the "think" step

Self-Talk

1. Tell myself, "I know it's not true." Tell myself, "They're just trying to make me mad and I won't let them." Tell myself, "I won't get into trouble because of what you're doing."

2. I ignore it. If I get asked about it, explain my side in a calm, quiet voice.

3. Tell myself that I don't always get to do what I want.

4. Tell myself, "They're trying to get me mad and I won't let them. " Tell myself, "They want me to get mad and I won't."

5. Ask for help until I understand it.

6. Tell myself, "Sometimes things aren't fair, I don't want to get into trouble."

7. Tell myself, "I'm important and I'll make a different friend."

8. Talk to someone I trust about my feelings.

Activity Sheet

Cut each scenario into strips to fold and have each child pick one out of an envelope or hat.

- -

1. When someone says a bad thing about me.

- -

2. When someone tattles on me.

- -

3. When I don't get to do what I want.

- -

4. When someone teases me.

- -

5. When I try hard and still get it wrong.

- -

6. When something isn't fair.

- -

7. When I feel left out.

- -

8. When I feel sad about something.

Stoplight Handout

Homework Sheet

Write down 3 times when you got mad and breathed.

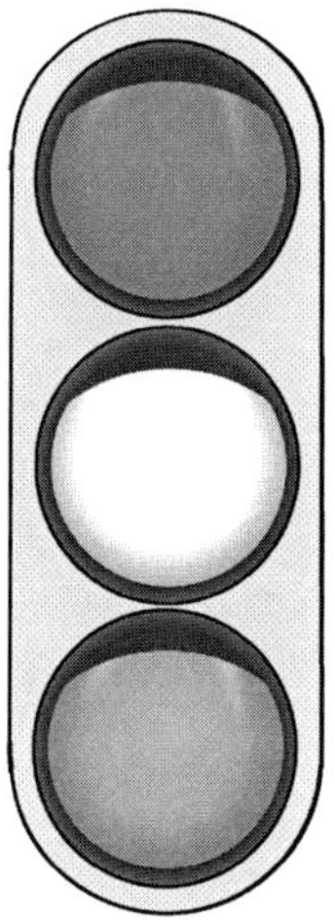

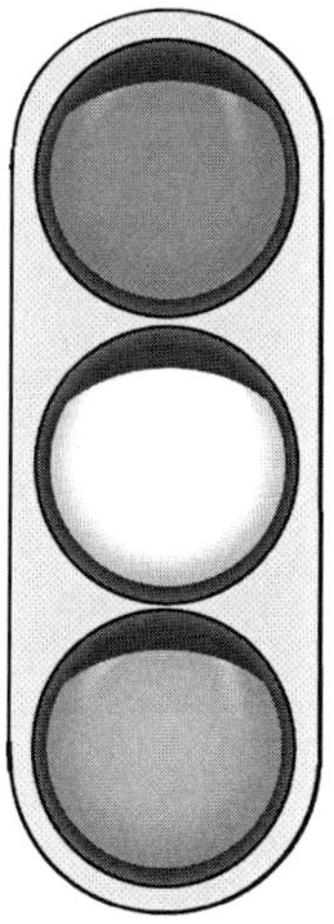

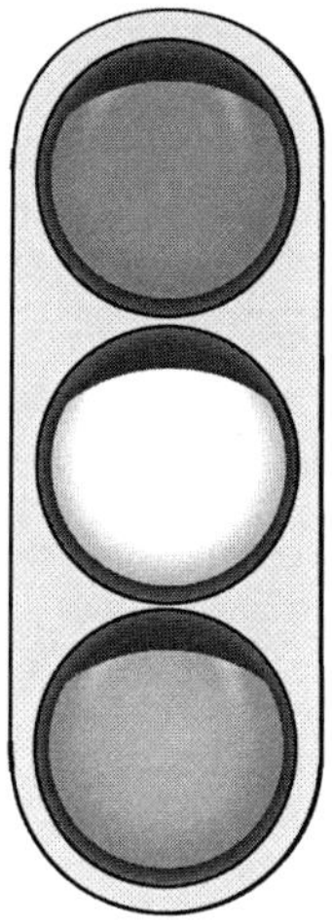

_____

_____

_____

_____

_____

_____

_____

Session *Five*

Goal

To help children formulate a plan of action.

Materials

1. Session 5 Stories. *page 62*
2. Session 5 Scenarios. *page 64*
3. Session 5 Game Board (reproducible sheet), pair of dice, pencils or crayons. *page 65*
4. Session 5 Homework Sheet. *page 66*

Procedure

1. Review homework

2. Mini-Lecture

After the discussion, say, "We're going to review from last week." Say, "We've learned that red means to stop, that yellow means to think and now we'll talk about green, which means to go. It's important to go in a way that will not get you into trouble. Three easy rules to remember are: No Shouting No Pouting No Doubting" Say, "No shouting means don't shout or do anything to hurt someone or destroy anything. No pouting means don't whine or pout or try to get the person to feel sorry for you. No doubting means speak in a clear, strong voice that says you're proud of yourself.

3. TemperTamer Stories

Read Session 5 stories and discuss them using the discussion questions.

4. Activity

Hand out a Session 5 game board to everyone (this is a reproducible sheet found at the end of this section). The object of the game is to mark off as many of the 12 squares as possible (with pencil or crayon). Taking turns, the children throw the dice. If they throw a 4 and a 2, they can mark off either the 4 or the 2 or add them to make 6 and mark off the 6. Before they mark it off they have to think of an appropriate response to either Scenario 4, 2, or 6 (depending on which one they choose) that you read to them. *For example, if they choose 2, you would read Scenario #2, which is: A kid you loaned your necklace to won't give it back.* They then have to verbalize an appropriate response to how they should handle the situation. The game continues in this manner until time runs out.

5. Homework

Ask the children to write down 3 times when they got mad and thought of a plan.

TemperTamer Stories

Story 1

Jacob keeps it cool

Jacob loved to play outside after school. But lately his mom had started to check if he had done his homework first. If he hadn't, he had to finish it before he went outside to play. Math was the worst. He hated it because it was so hard for him. Today, when he got home, two of his friends were already on their bikes and he wanted to go with them.

"C'mon Jacob," they said. "Get your bike and we'll meet you in five minutes."

Jacob said, "OK," and went inside.

But his mom was waiting for him. She said, "Jacob, finish your snack quick so we can do your math before you go to your dad's for the night.

"Mom," Jacob shouted, "I don't want to do homework now." Why did he have to be the only one whose mom made him stay in? And why did he have to go to his dad's house tonight? The more he thought the madder he got. Finally, he got so mad he started stomping his feet and kicking the kitchen chair. He was about to start screaming out loud and he didn't think he could stop himself.

"Wait a minute," his Mom said. "Remember what you learned in group? Now you need to stop and take a deep breath and another one and then make a plan so that you don't do anything that will get you into worse trouble. I really don't want to have to ground you. And I'm sure you don't want to be grounded." Jacob nodded his head yes. So he took some deep breaths, like he learned in "Cool Club," and thought of a plan. He really wanted to play with his friends because he would miss them all weekend. He went to his room for a little bit and when he came out he asked his mom about a plan he had thought up. He used his calm, quiet voice to ask her. "Mom, I really want to play now because I won't get to all weekend at Dad's. Could I please do my homework on Sunday night when I come back?" His mom thought for awhile and said, "All right, I know how much you want to play now so I will let you go and then when you get back you will have to do your homework and not watch TV at all." Jacob said "OK," right away and raced out the door to catch his friends.

Discussion

1. Why did Jacob get mad?

2. How did he stop from doing something which would have gotten him into trouble?

TemperTamer Stories

Story 2

Alicia the Brat

Shanika hated having to babysit her little sister Alicia, because she never listened. Today her mom told her, "You have to watch Alicia after school because I have to work late." So here she was again, stuck watching Alicia the Brat. Shanika wanted to watch the "Simpsons" on TV, but Alicia was being such a brat. She kept turning the channel to dumb old "Mary Kate and Ashley." Finally Shanika had enough. She was holding the channel changer up high so Alicia couldn't grab it and Alicia was starting to scream like she always did when she didn't get her way. She screamed and screamed until Shanika couldn't stand it any longer.

Suddenly, Shanika remembered what she learned about the "stoplight." Let's see, she thought, how did that go? If she slowed herself down and took a deep breath, maybe she wouldn't do anything to her sister that would get her into trouble with her mom. She already got into a lot of trouble when she threatened to beat up Alicia for tattling on her. Shanika stopped and breathed deeply and then got away from Alicia by going into her room and listening to the radio. When their mom came home, Alicia was still screaming and trying to get into Shanika's room. Mom started shouting and said, "What is going on here? I thought I told you to watch your sister for me. Why can't I trust you two?" She looked at Shanika and said, "And you . . . you are older and should be more responsible." Shanika thought, "Oh no, I'm in trouble again and I'll get grounded." But she took another deep breath and tried to explain exactly what happened. When she was done, her mom said, "You know, I think you did the right thing by just getting away and not hurting your sister. I am proud of you because I can see that you are working hard at controlling your temper. I'll have to see if I can get home sooner so you girls aren't home alone so much."

Discussion

1. What made Shanika mad?

2. List the things Shanika did to keep herself from getting into trouble.

Session 5 Scenarios

Each student has his or her own game board. As the dice are thrown, each student marks off the number that is thrown so that number is taken. He responds to his scenario before the second child throws his dice. When a scenario is taken, throw again.

Each student throws either one or two die and lands on one of the following 12 scenarios:

❑ 1. A girl who sits next to you makes a face at you and writes "I hate you" on a piece of paper and shows it to you.

❑ 2. A kid you loaned your necklace to won't give it back.

❑ 3. You're riding in the car and your brother keeps changing the radio station you like.

❑ 4. Your teacher thinks you took something but you didn't.

❑ 5. Your mom forgets to buy you the treat that you wanted.

❑ 6. Your dad says you can't go outside until you clean your room.

❑ 7. A boy shoves you as you're getting on the bus.

❑ 8. Your mom gets mad and yells at you.

❑ 9. A kid on the playground is bossy and has to have everything his way.

❑ 10. Your little sister broke the gum ball machine you got as a present.

❑ 11. Your brother broke the Nintendo 64 controller.

❑ 12. You didn't get your worksheet done and you have to stay in during recess.

Game Board

3

2

4

1

Start Here

5

6

7

8

Finish Here

12

9

11

10

Homework Sheet

Write down 3 times when you got mad and thought of a plan.

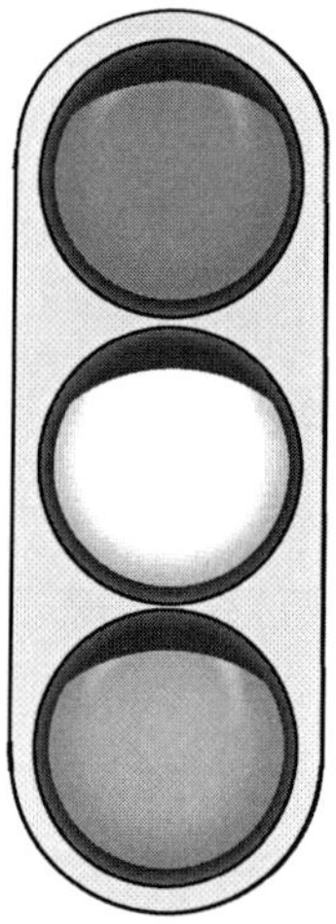

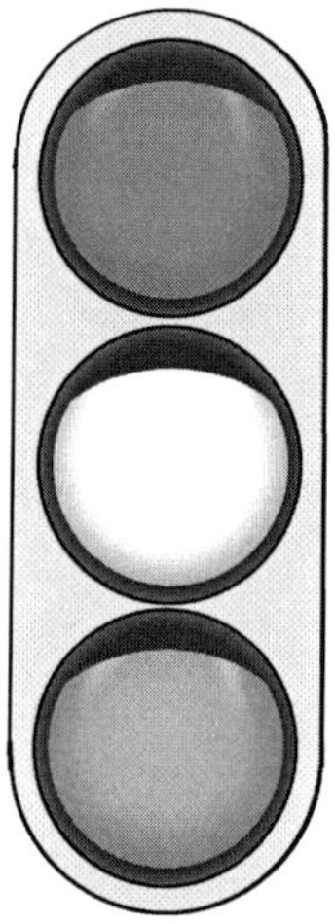

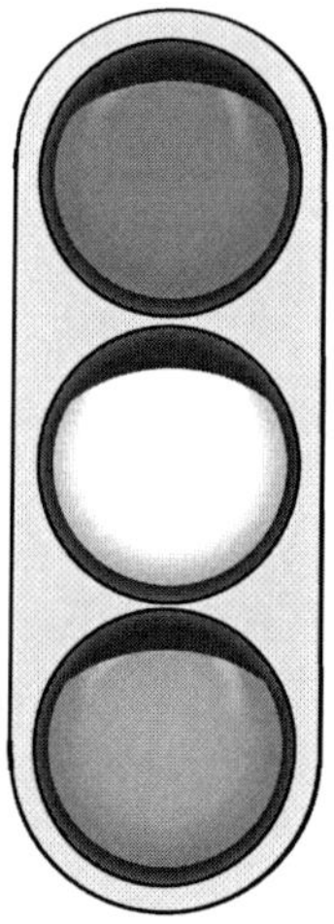

_____

_____

_____

_____

_____

_____

_____

_____

_____

Session
Six

Goal

To help children carry out the plan.

Materials

1. Session 6 Stories. *page 70*

2. Session 6 Scenarios. *page 73*

3. Session 6 "Shout or Pout" cards. Make these ahead of time by reproducing the "Shout" and "Pout" page and cutting them into cards. *page 72*

4. Session 6 Homework Sheet. *page 74*

Procedure

1. Review homework

2. Mini-Lecture

Say, "Last time we talked about what we should do when something made us mad. First we think of the stoplight and stop and breathe, right? Next we think of a plan and then the last part is to do the plan. Even when we are mad, we don't want to shout or do something to hurt someone or destroy anything. We also don't want to whine or pout and feel sorry for ourselves or try to get someone else to feel sorry for us."

3. Mini-Lecture

Say, "Let's read these stories and see what these kids did."

4. TemperTamer Stories

Read stories, discuss them using the discussion questions, read the second ending and discuss.

5. Activity

Leader has the "Shout/Pout" cards in hand, with the blank side facing the children. ("Shout" and "Pout" cards are on page 72.) Each student is instructed to pick one of the cards, which will either have "shout" or "pout" on it. The students are then told they will have to make up a reaction, either one that is "Shouting" or "Pouting" in response to a scenario that is read to them. (It has been my experience that this role playing is difficult for children, but with coaching they can get into it.) After each child completes the "Shout or Pout" role play, ask for an example of the correct way to handle the situation.

6. Homework

Put down 3 times when you got mad but didn't shout or pout.

TemperTamer Stories

Mini-Lecture say, "These stories are different because they have more than one ending."

Story 1

Tyrone and the Bully

As Tyrone was getting on the school bus, he groaned, "Oh, no," to himself, because he saw that mean kid sitting there again. The kid was new and he was a bully. Yesterday, when Tyrone got on the bus, the kid made faces and stuck his leg out, making him trip. Today, the mean kid had that evil look in his eyes again. As soon as Tyrone sat down he laughed and reached over the seat to grab Tyrone's backpack. He said he wasn't going to give it back.

Ending 1

Tyrone was so mad he didn't remember to stop himself and he yelled and punched the kid in the face. Mr. Gorman, the driver, saw him punch the mean kid, so he said he would turn in a bus report on Tyrone.

Discussion

1. Who got into trouble?

2. Why?

Ending 2

Tyrone was so mad he almost started to cry. He put his head down and wouldn't look at the kid or anyone else on the bus. When the bus got to school and everybody piled out of their seats, Tyrone walked slowly with his head down. He knew it was going to be a miserable day.

Discussion

1. Would Tyrone have a very good day?

2. Would Tyrone's behavior stop the kid from picking on him on him the next day?

3. What would be a better ending for the story?

TemperTamer Stories

Story 2

The Reading Contest

Chris was almost done reading a book he'd checked out of the library. Although, he rather be outside playing, and it was a perfect day, he'd spent it reading in his room. You see, Chris's class was having a contest and the student who read the most books would win a really cool calculator watch. And Chris wanted to be that student.

When he finally finished the book, he got the book chart out of his backpack and marked down "Alien Werewolf," in the space. That was number 47. That's a lot, he thought. He should win for sure because he didn't think anyone else read as many books as he did.

Since he was done reading, Chris went to play Nintendo. But his sister Cindy was already playing. He was so sick of reading he really wanted to play, so he pushed her out of the way and grabbed the controllers.

Cindy got so mad she ran out of the room shouting, "I'm gonna get you back." The next thing he knew, Chris saw Cindy running into her room with his backpack. I'm gonna tear up your homework," she shouted, "it'll serve you right."

By the time Chris got to her room, she had the book list in her hand. As he reached out to stop her from ripping it, she pulled in the other direction. The next thing he heard was "r-r-r-rip." The list he worked so hard on and needed to turn in tomorrow was torn right down the middle.

Ending 1

Chris blew up! He grabbed Cindy by her shoulders and started shouting at her. The more he shouted the madder he got.

He wanted to get even with her so badly he punched her and ran into her room to find something of hers to break. His mom came running into Cindy's room because she heard the commotion. "Christopher," she yelled, "you are in such big trouble!"

Discussion

1. Who was his mom most mad at?

2. Who would get into the most trouble?

Ending 2

Chris thought, "Oh no, nothing I ever do comes out right. Now I can't turn in the sheet and I won't win even though I read the most books. I think I'll just stay home from school tomorrow because it won't be a fun day for me at all."

Discussion

1. Is Chris making the right decision to give up his chances of winning and not go to school at all?

2. What would be a better ending for the story?

Activity Sheet

Shout	Pout
Shout	Pout
Shout	Pout
Shout	Pout

Session 6 Scenarios

1. A kid in your class is jealous and told your friends lies about you. As a result your best friend ditches you.

2. There are kids on your bus who are bullies. They pick on other kids until they feel hurt or explode in anger. These kids start to pick on you on the bus.

3. Sometimes you get along with your brother, sometimes you don't. Today he's being a real jerk and is teasing you about everything.

4. Everyone in your family has been busy and hasn't had time to do the chores. There's a whole pile of dirty dishes in the kitchen sink but you don't think it's your job, so when you get home from school you turn on the TV and sit down to watch your favorite shows. When your mom gets home, she says you have to do them before she can start making supper.

5. Your class has been working on making memory books. A parent volunteer is there, helping kids use the laminator. You just have one part left to finish on your book, but the teacher is telling everyone to put their work away. You don't want your book laminated because it isn't done, but the teacher is telling everyone they have to finish up right now.

6. Your brother and you are using the PlayStation. He always seems to win. He wins again because he killed the last of your guys.

7. Along with your three best friends, you start a club. Another friend who isn't in the club writes a note to your three friends, saying you shouldn't be in the club. You just finished reading the note.

8. You're playing kick ball outside during recess and you kick it too high by accident, lose your balance and fall down. Everyone laughs and you hear one kid say, "loser."

Homework Sheet

Write down 3 times when you got mad but didn't shout or pout.

Shout

Pout

Shout

Session *Seven*

Goal

To help children be assertive.

Materials

1. Session 7 Stories. *page 78*
2. Session 7 Homework Sheet. *page 80*

Procedure

1. Review homework

2. Mini-Lecture

Say, "Last time we learned about wrong ways to handle situations when we got mad. What is the easy rule to remember? No Shouting and No Pouting. Today we are going to learn how to be strong and how to not doubt ourselves. The first thing we want to do is to ACT STRONG by:

a. standing or sitting straight
b. looking the person in the eye

The next thing we want to do is to SPEAK STRONG by:
a. saying what you want
b. saying what will happen next . . ."

3. TemperTamer Stories

Say, "Let's see how these kids acted strong." Read Session 7 stories and ask the discussion questions. Say, "Lets read the stories and see how these kids acted strong."

4. Have each child pair up with a partner.

Say, "We're going to practice acting strong by having everyone take turns and sit or stand straight and look their partner in the eye." Have them practice.

5. Activity

Get back into the group. Say, "Now we're going to practice speaking strong. What are some things that might happen to make you mad?" If the children have a hard time thinking of situations, some examples are:

a. someone kicking their chair
b. someone cutting in front of them
c. someone taking something from them
d. someone hurting them
e. someone yelling at them
f. someone teasing them
g. someone laughing at them

Say, "To speak strong, say what you want or what you don't like, and say what will happen next. For example: "I want you to stop kicking my chair or I will tell the teacher." To finish the discussion say, "Sometimes the person doesn't stop, but you just need to walk away or tell yourself, 'It's not worth getting in trouble over,' so you don't do anything that gets you in trouble."

6. Homework

Children must put down 3 times when they spoke strong and acted strong.

TemperTamer Stories

Story 1

Charles Keeps His Cool

Charles could hardly wait for recess. The last two days it had been raining and the whole school had to stay inside during recess. It was so boring inside! They could only play quiet board games in the school.

But today it was sunny and Charles wanted to play soccer. He was a pretty good kicker because he had been practicing. Finally, his teacher, Mr. Adamson, said, "Okay class, it's time to go out for recess." Everyone cheered, "Yea!"

Everyone crowded to get in line because they were excited about going out. Charles was behind Carrie and in front of Mark. Mark shoved Charles who couldn't stop himself from bumping into Carrie who got hurt and started to cry.

Mr. Adamson looked right at Charles and said, "All right, that's enough. You don't get to go out for recess today. You march right down to the principal's office." Charles was so mad he started to boil over.

He was just about to turn around and yell at Mark. But before he did he remembered the stoplight. Just in time he stopped himself from yelling, or worse, kicking Mark. Instead, he made himself be still, he took a breath and made a plan.

Charles decided to go to the principal's office and use his quiet voice to explain what happened. When he got there, Mrs. Petrie, the principal, saw him come in and said, "Charles, what are you here for?"

He told her the whole story in a calm voice. When he was done she said, "I think I'll ask Mr. Adamson to send Mark down so we can have a little talk, because it doesn't seem like it was your fault. Why don't you put your jacket on and go outside so you can still have a chance to be out before it's time to come in."

So Charles went to his locker, got his jacket and ran outside in time to see that his class was still playing soccer. He ran over to join them and his friend Andy said, "Hey Charles, play on our side, we're winning." So he did, he had a great time . . . AND his team won.

Discussion

1. Why did Charles get so mad?

2. Was it his fault that he got sent to the principal's office?

3. What did he do so that he didn't get into trouble?

TemperTamer Stories

Story 2

The Trouble with Younger Brothers . . .

Lindsey was spending the night. Jenny's mom said Lindsey could stay over if they both kept an eye on her little brother Jeremy until she got home from work. But Jeremy was so annoying. When Jenny had friends over he never stopped showing off and bothering them.

This always got Jenny in trouble because she'd lose her temper and hit him. Then Jeremy would run bawling like a baby to their parents. As soon as Lindsey arrived, Jeremy started right in bugging them. Every few minutes he'd pop in and throw dumb things, like his fuzzy soccer ball, into Jenny's room.

Jenny was starting to lose it but she didn't want to blow the chance to have friends stay over by losing her temper and pounding her bratty brother. So she decided to go to the doorway and talk to Jeremy. But, the minute she opened the door, Jeremy took off giggling like crazy. Jenny ran after him and he just thought that was a great game.

She finally caught Jeremy in the kitchen and trapped him by the sink. But instead of hitting him she said in her quiet voice, "I'm tired of you trying to make me mad everytime I have a friend over. If you don't stop I will keep track every time you throw something and I'll tell Mom when she comes home."

But Jeremy wasn't used to her talking calmly, so he didn't believe Jenny and kept on trying to bug her. Still, Jenny tried really hard to keep her temper. And she did. When her mom came home, she told her all the things he had done. Boy, was her mom mad at Jeremy.

Discussion

1. Did Jenny's behavior change what her little brother was doing?

2. What will help Jeremy change his behavior?

3. Would it help for them to just keep on fighting?

4. Will Jenny lose her chance to have a friend over for doing what she did?

Homework Sheet

Write down 3 times when you got mad and you acted strong and spoke strong.

Strong

Strong

Strong

Session *Eight*

Goal

To review and to help children learn how to get rid of angry energy.

Materials

1. Session 8 Stories. *page 84*

Procedure

1. Review homework

2. TemperTamer Stories/Activity

Say, "For the activity today, we need some volunteers to be in some plays." Scan the story to ask for appropriate volunteers: i.e., story number 1 needs a boy, "Josh," a "teacher" and some "kids."
The children actually do very little acting. Instead, they pantomime a bit while the group leader reads the story with inflection. However, most of them really enjoy the chance to perform.

When the story is done, include the group in the discussion questions.

3. Mini-Lecture

Say, "We've been talking all along about how to control our tempers so we don't do anything to get ourselves into trouble. We've learned how to handle situations in ways that are strong and positive.
We haven't talked about what to do if we still have a lot of energy left in our bodies after we've done all that we could. Sometimes anger gives us a lot of energy and it's still left even after we breath and handle the situation." Ask, "What are some ways you can get rid of the energy that you still might feel?" Examples include: Walking, running, jumping, bicycling, roller blading, swimming, etc.

Say, "Some people also let off energy and calm down by doing things like: Reading a book, watching TV, playing a video game, writing their thoughts down, drawing, coloring."

End the group by asking for volunteers to suggest some activities they might choose to do in an enclosed space such as: Sit-ups, push-ups, running in place, hopping, or any other kind of physical activity that can be safely done in a contained space. As time permits, allow a volunteer to lead the group in this activity.

TemperTamer Stories

Story 1

The Loud Teacher

Josh's teacher told the class to put their reading away and get out a piece of paper. Josh wanted to finish the story in his reading book because he wasn't done yet.

He kept on reading when suddenly he saw the teacher was standing right next to him. The teacher said in a loud voice, "What did I just tell you to do?" The loud voice made Josh jump and then he got really mad because the whole class was staring at him and starting to laugh. He could feel he was getting angry inside.

Discussion

1. What can Josh do first to keep himself from losing his temper?

2. What can he say next, without shouting or pouting?

TemperTamer Stories

Story 2

The Dirty Nail Polish

Angelina had told her sister she could use her new glitter nail polish. She had been begging and whining and Angelina really didn't want to let her because she had bought it with her birthday money. But her sister was such a pest she finally said she'd let her. Her sister took the bottle and brought it outside. Angelina didn't want her using it outside because she was worried she might get dirt in it or something. Her sister carefully started putting the polish on her nails. She had almost finished doing her left hand when their dog Puffy rushed out of the garage and spilled the polish all over the ground. Angelina was so mad.

Discussion

1. How can Angelina control her temper?

2. How can she let her sister know that she's mad without shouting or pouting?

3. What could she suggest that would be a fair payback for the spilled bottle of nail polish?

TemperTamer Stories

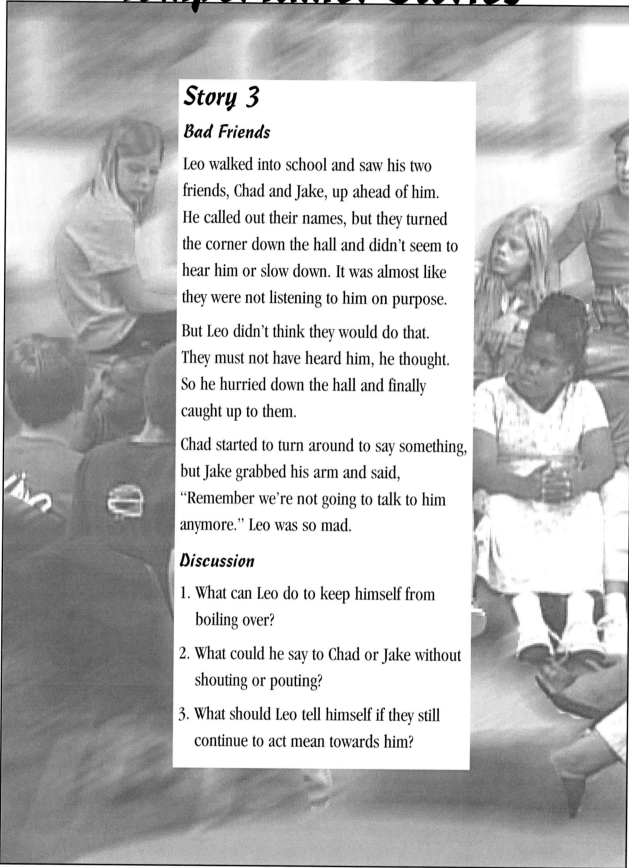

Story 3

Bad Friends

Leo walked into school and saw his two
friends, Chad and Jake, up ahead of him.
He called out their names, but they turned
the corner down the hall and didn't seem to
hear him or slow down. It was almost like
they were not listening to him on purpose.

But Leo didn't think they would do that.
They must not have heard him, he thought.
So he hurried down the hall and finally
caught up to them.

Chad started to turn around to say something,
but Jake grabbed his arm and said,
"Remember we're not going to talk to him
anymore." Leo was so mad.

Discussion

1. What can Leo do to keep himself from
   boiling over?

2. What could he say to Chad or Jake without
   shouting or pouting?

3. What should Leo tell himself if they still
   continue to act mean towards him?

TemperTamer Stories

Story 4

The Cheater

Ramon and Richardo were playing table tennis. Richardo was winning and he was happy. Ramon was a bad sport and he hated to lose. He always thought he was the best at everything. Richardo only had to win this last serve and he would win the game.

Richardo served and Ramon smacked the ball as hard as he could. It went right over Ramon's head, where it slammed into the wall and broke.

Richardo started to say that he won and Ramon said, "No you didn't, the ball has a crack in it and we have to play over with another ball." Richardo knew that Ramon was cheating and he was getting very mad.

Discussion

1. What can Richardo do first to control his temper?

2. What can he say to Ramon to let him know that he is mad without shouting or pouting?

Story 5

Fat Picture

Roxanne didn't like the new girl, Portia. She seemed to want to take over all of Roxanne's friends. Roxanne knew her friends liked her but lately they weren't treating her the way they used to.

It made Roxanne wonder if the new girl was saying bad things about her. During recess she saw a bunch of kids standing over by the slide and the new girl was showing them a picture she had drawn of Roxanne.

The picture made Roxanne look fat and terrible. Everyone, even her friends, were laughing. Roxanne felt herself getting very angry.

Discussion

1. What's the first thing Roxanne can do to keep from losing her temper?

2. What can Roxanne say, without shouting or pouting to let people know that she is mad?

TemperTamer Stories

Story 6

Not Fair

Joey's brother was on the PlayStation and Joey really wanted to play. His brother had been playing for at least half an hour and Joey said it was his turn. "All right, all right," his brother said. "Just wait 'till I kill this one guy." Joey thought, "Oh no, now I'll never get on." His brother finally killed the guy and Joseph got on to play. Just then his dad called, "Come on now, it's time to eat and I want you two here right now!" Joey was so mad.

Discussion

1. What's the first thing Joey can do to keep from losing his temper?

2. What can he say to his brother and his dad so that they know that he's mad, without shouting or pouting?

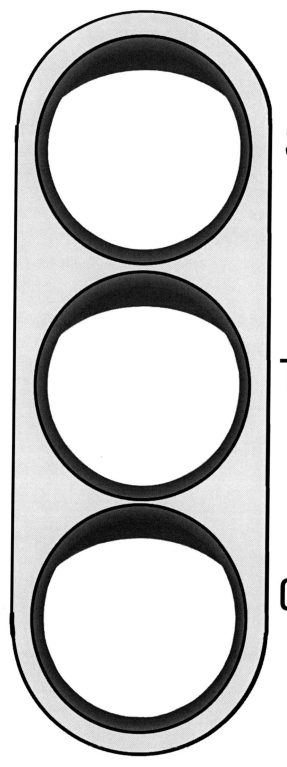

Stop and breathe

Think and plan

Go – Do the plan

Additional Reproducible

NO Shouting

NO Pouting

NO Doubting

Act Strong

Speak Strong

Appendix

Feeling Faces

The following full page "feeling faces" can be reproduced and put up on your bulletin board to highlight a "feeling" of the week, or sent home with students to review with their parents.

*(**editor's note:** Kathryn Pearson, a licensed psychologist and the author of this program says of the following images: "Visuals are a vital component in helping kids understand more about their emotions. Take note that the facial expression of some feelings are virtually interchangeable, for example, frustrated vs. stressed, sad vs. disappointed. Point this out to your students when introducing this concept. This is useful information that allows them to become more 'emotionally intelligent' and to better control their tempers."*

Tereza Snyder, Senior Software Developer for Attainment Company, Inc. created the TemperTamer images. Snyder is a B.F.A. graduate of Parsons Schools of Design in New York and an M.F.A. candidate at the University of Wisconsin-Madison.

Of her images, she says: "I created the faces using **The Artist's Complete Guide to Facial Expression** by Gary Faigin (1990; Watson-Guptil Publications; ISBN 0-8230-1628-5) as a guide. My aim was to strike a balance between stylization and accurate naturalism by emphasizing the critical features of expression: The eyes, brows, mouth and wrinkles, while flattening and simplifying nonessential aspects; hair, ears and nose. Although all faces are entirely imaginary, I tried to make each one look like a specific individual."

Calm

loving

happy

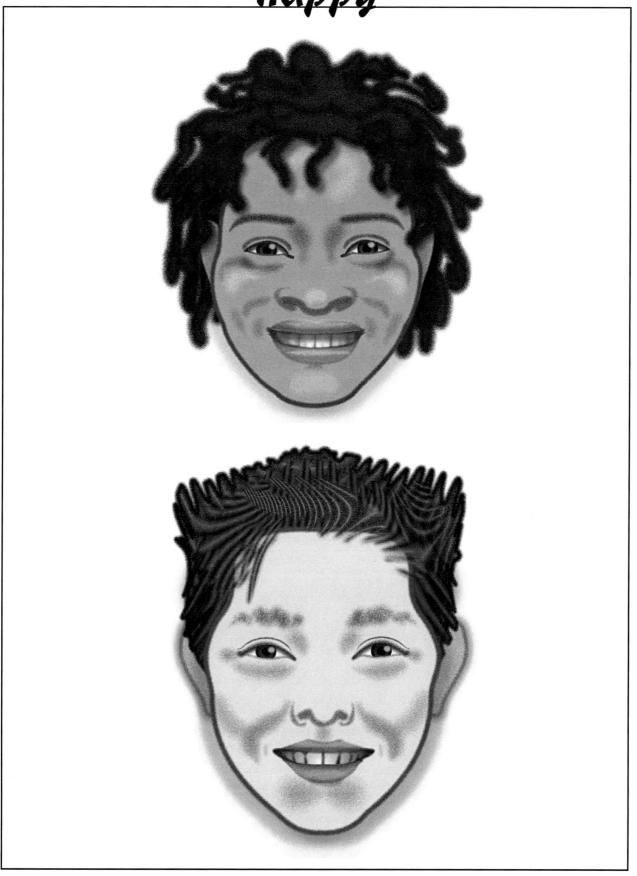

proud

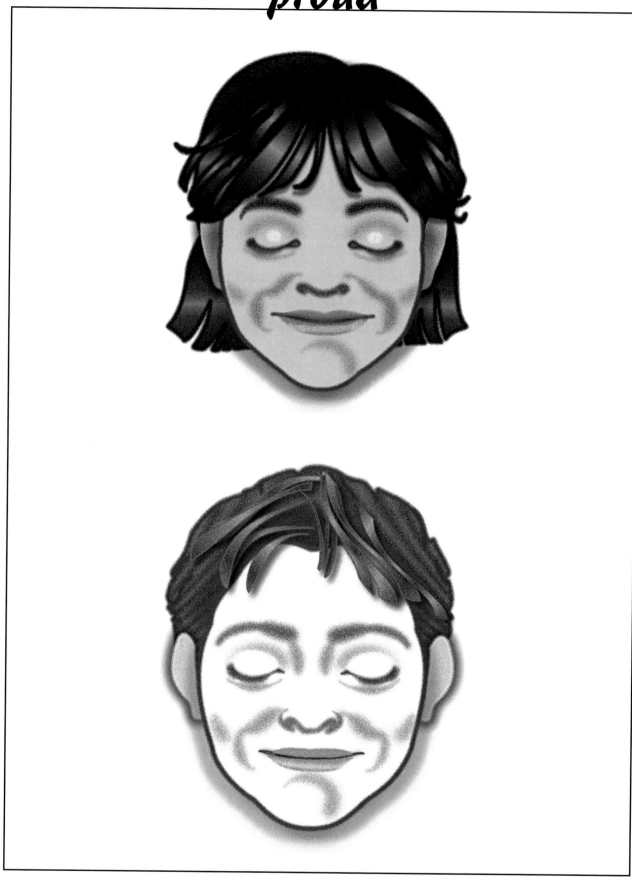

excited

surprised

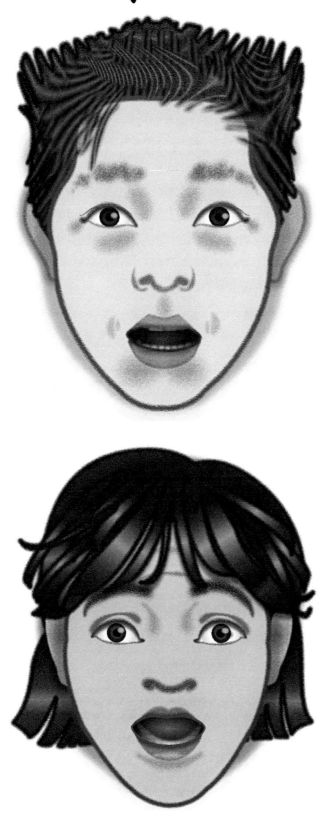

shy

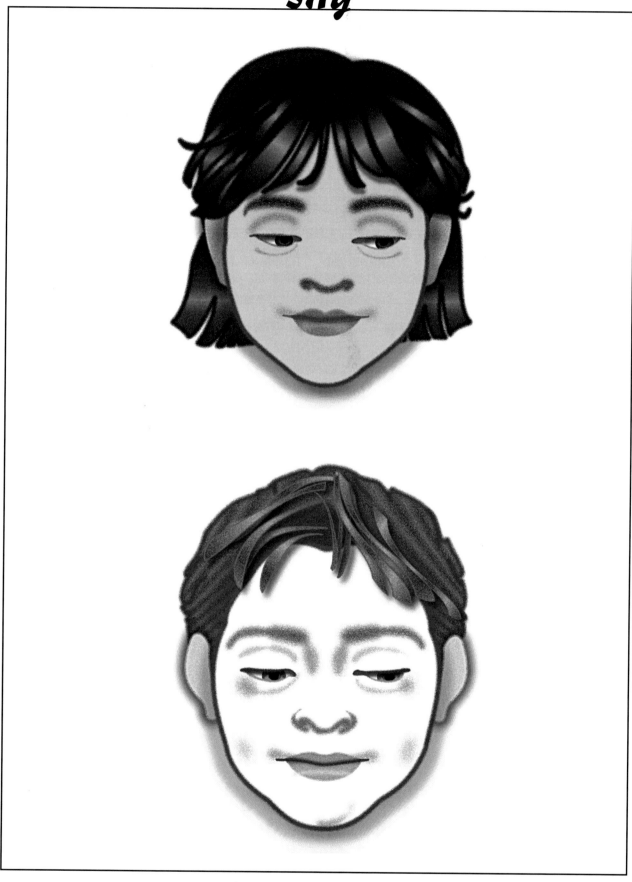

bored

worried

confused

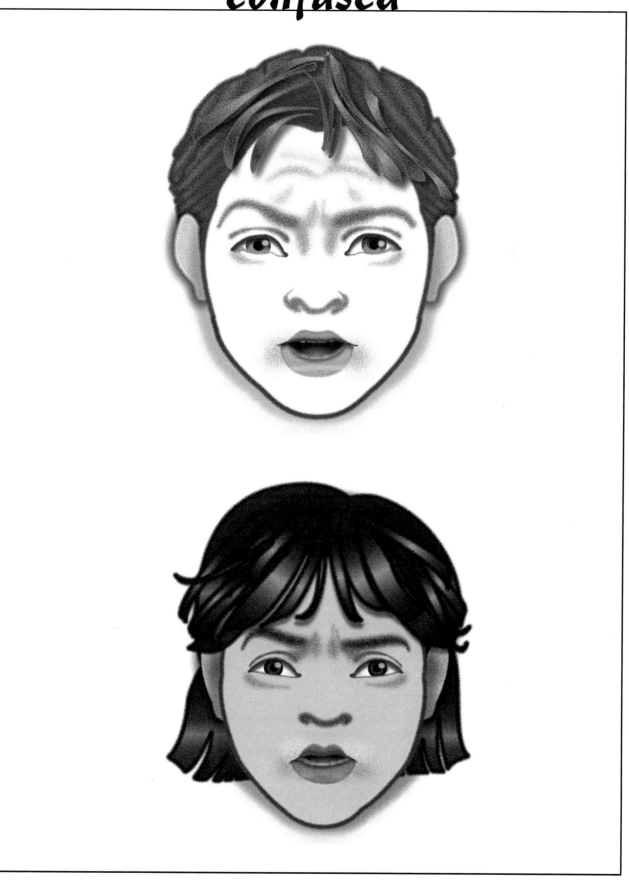

lonely

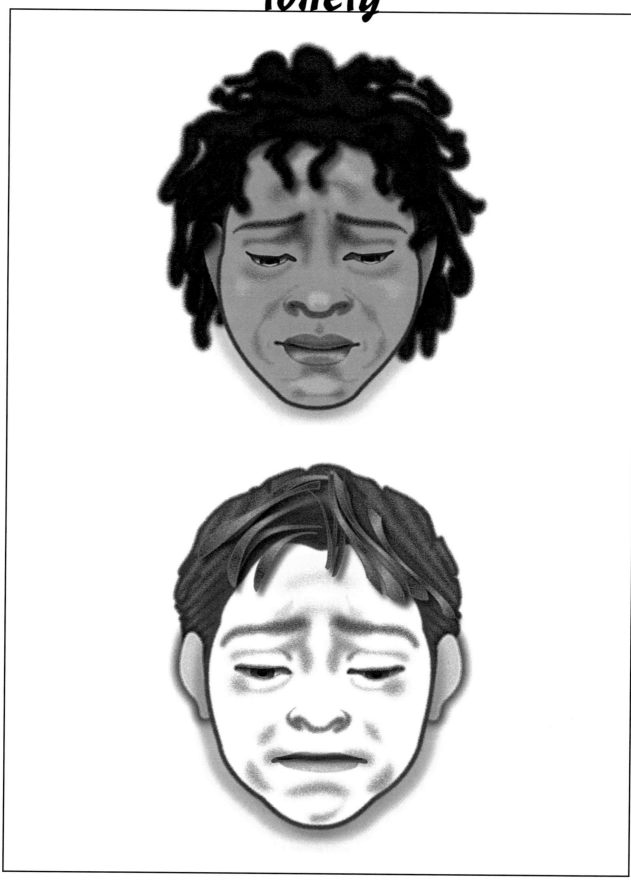

disappointed

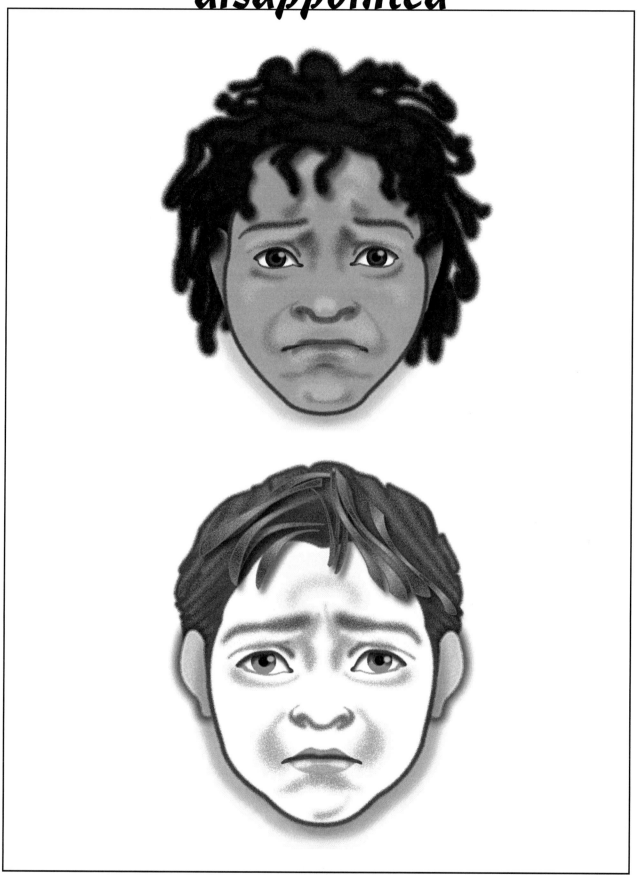

upset

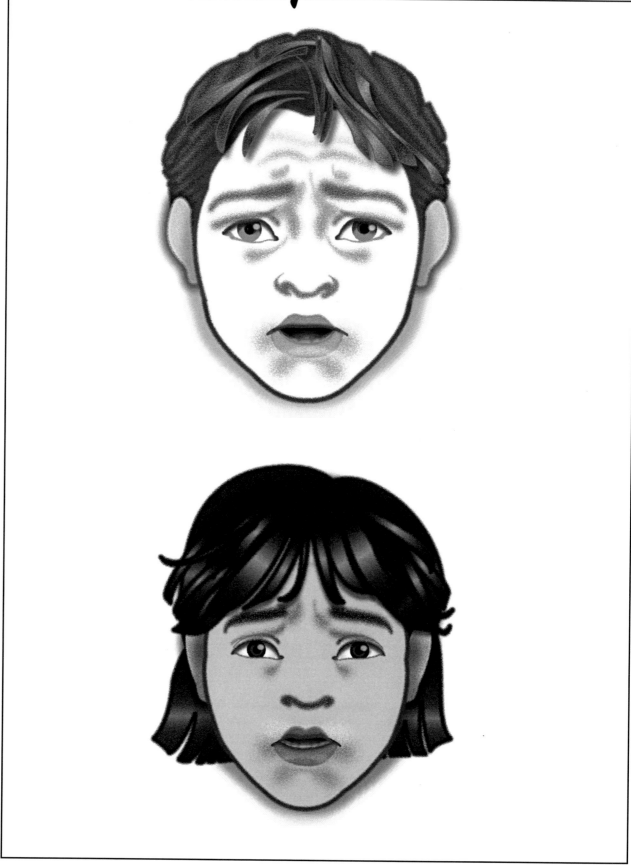

embarrassed

sad

mad

annoyed

stressed

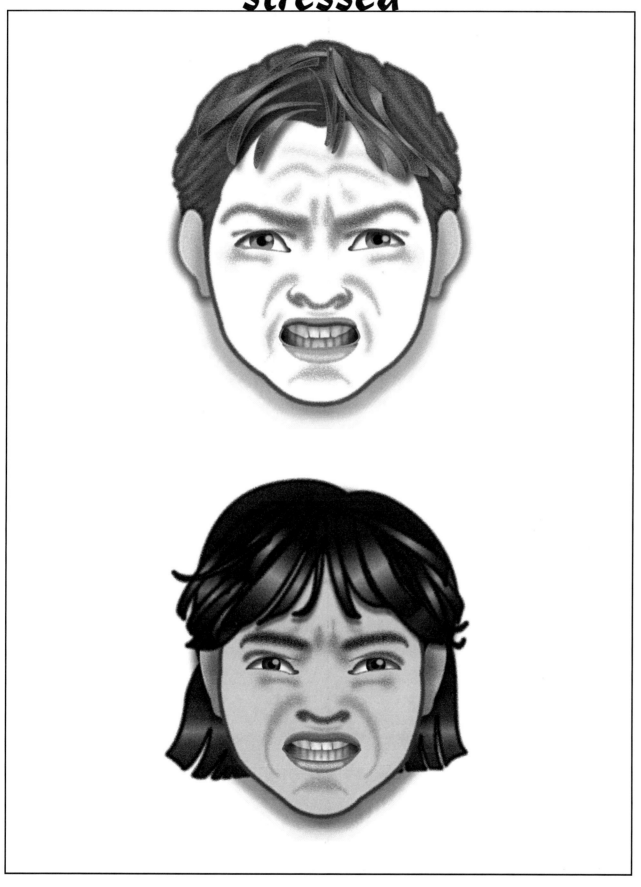

frustrated

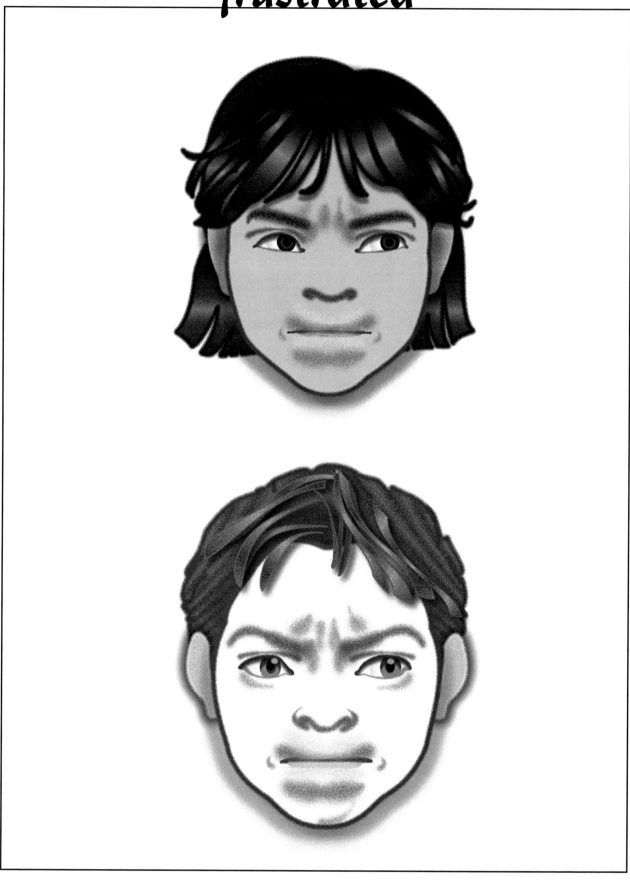

scared

rejected

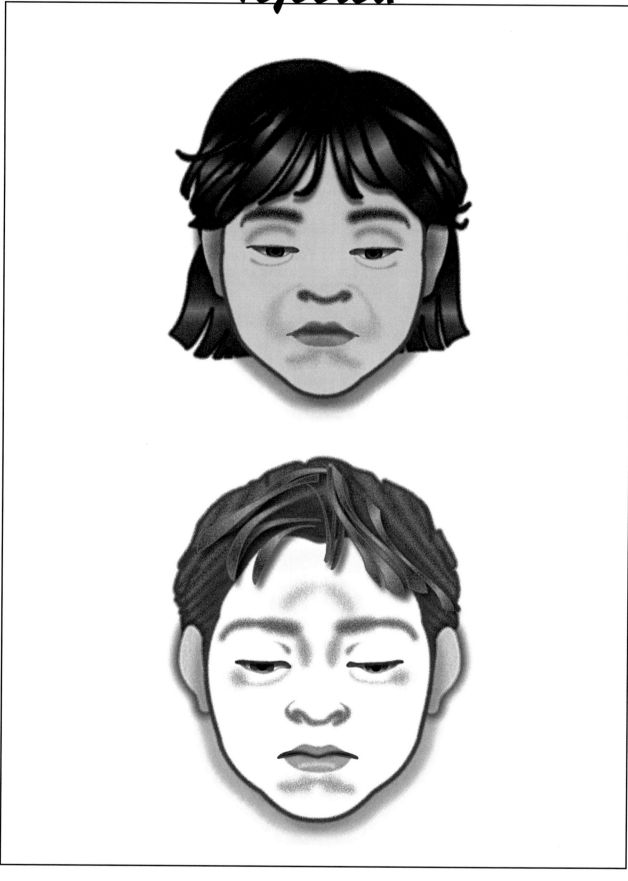

jealous

nervous

guilty

furious

relieved